BLINKY-BUGS!

MAKE YOUR OWN ELECTRIC INSECTS

BY
KEN MURPHY

ILLUSTRATED BY
ALEXANDER TARRANT

chronicle books · san francisco

FOR MY WICKED AWESOME NEPHEW, AARON —K. M.

TEXT © 2010 BY KEN MURPHY.
ILLUSTRATIONS AND PHOTOS © 2010 BY CHRONICLE BOOKS LLC.

COVER DESIGN BY MARK NEELY.
DESIGN BY NATALIE DAVIS.
TYPESET IN DIGITAL STRIP.

ISBN 978-0-8118-7140-2

MANUFACTURED BY LEO PAPER PRODUCTS,
HESHAN, CHINA, IN JUNE 2010.

1 3 5 7 9 10 8 6 4 2

THIS PRODUCT CONFORMS TO ASTM
AND CPSIA 2008 SAFETY STANDARDS.

CHRONICLE BOOKS LLC
680 SECOND STREET
SAN FRANCISCO, CALIFORNIA 94107

WWW.CHRONICLEKIDS.COM

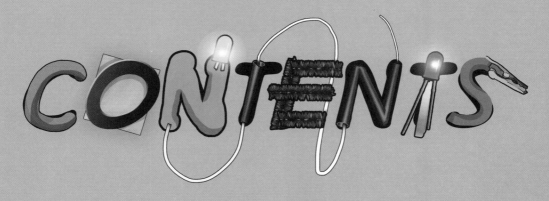

CONTENTS

WHEN BLINKYBUGS FEEL EVEN THE SLIGHTEST MOVEMENT— EVEN A LIGHT BREEZE—THEY RESPOND BY BLINKING THEIR EYES.

WHEN THE WIRES TOUCH, THE EYES LIGHT UP!

WHEN THE WIRES ARE NOT TOUCHING, THE EYES ARE OFF.

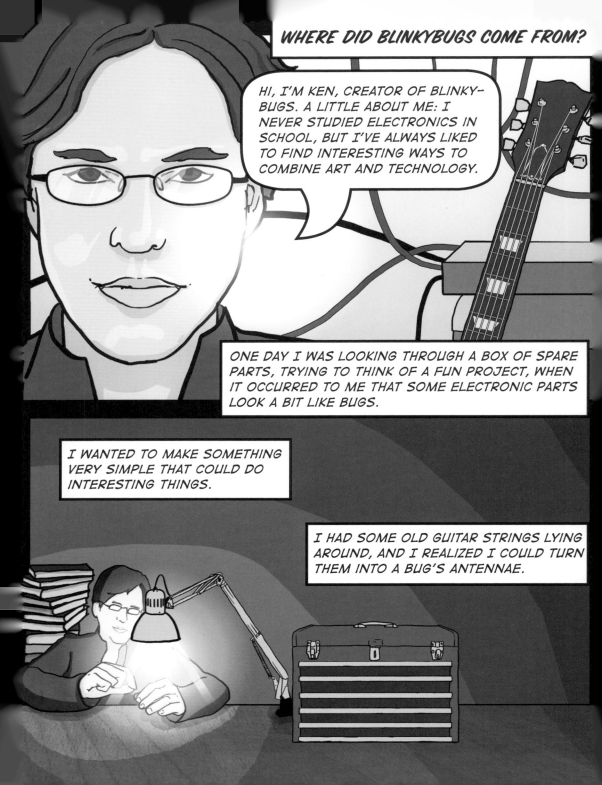

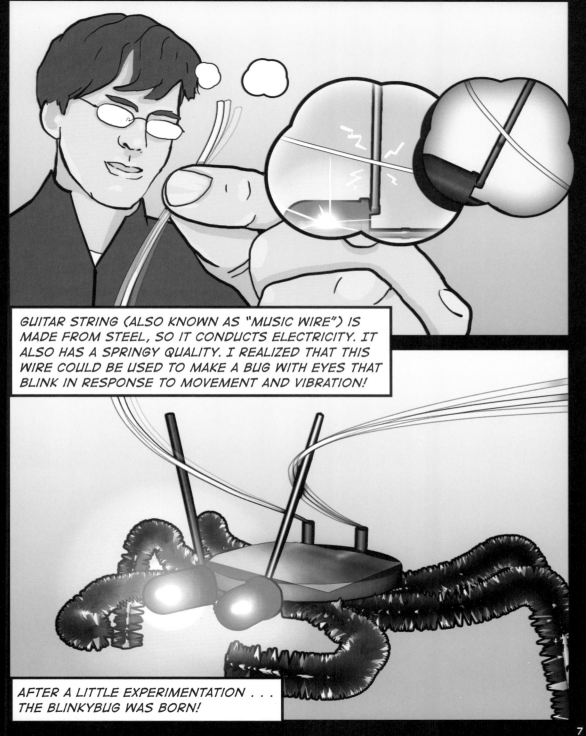

GUITAR STRING (ALSO KNOWN AS "MUSIC WIRE") IS MADE FROM STEEL, SO IT CONDUCTS ELECTRICITY. IT ALSO HAS A SPRINGY QUALITY. I REALIZED THAT THIS WIRE COULD BE USED TO MAKE A BUG WITH EYES THAT BLINK IN RESPONSE TO MOVEMENT AND VIBRATION!

AFTER A LITTLE EXPERIMENTATION . . . THE BLINKYBUG WAS BORN!

EVERYTHING YOU NEED TO MAKE A BLINKYBUG

KIT CONTENTS

- COIN-CELL BATTERIES (3)
- COLORED PIPE CLEANERS (3)
- COPPER TUBES (3)
- FOIL WITH CONDUCTIVE ADHESIVE, 2 X 3 INCHES (5 X 7 CM)
- GLUE DOTS (6)
- LEDS (2 EACH OF RED, YELLOW, AND GREEN)
- MUSIC WIRE, 3 PIECES, EACH 12 INCHES (30 CM)
- POM-POMS (3 LARGE AND 15 SMALL)
- FEATHERS

SAFETY

BLINKYBUGS ARE FAIRLY SAFE TO MAKE. STILL, SOME OF THE TOOLS CAN PINCH OR POKE, AND THE KIT INCLUDES SMALL PARTS THAT YOU SHOULD KEEP AWAY FROM YOUNGER KIDS WHO MIGHT PUT THEM IN THEIR MOUTHS. THROUGHOUT THE INSTRUCTIONS, ANY STEPS THAT REQUIRE SPECIAL ATTENTION TO SAFETY ARE INDICATED WITH THIS SYMBOL:

PREPARING PARTS

IF YOU ARE A YOUNGER BUG-MAKER, YOU MIGHT WANT TO ASK SOMEONE OLDER FOR HELP WITH SOME OF THE TRICKIER STEPS. ANOTHER OPTION IS TO ASK THEM TO PREPARE SOME OF THE PARTS FOR YOU IN ADVANCE. AND ALWAYS BE SURE TO HAVE PERMISSION FROM AN ADULT BEFORE BEGINNING YOUR PROJECT. CHALLENGING STEPS WILL HAVE THIS ICON AT LEFT NEXT TO THEM.

ALL ABOUT LED EYES

LEDS
LEDS, LIKE LIGHTBULBS, TURN ELECTRICAL ENERGY INTO LIGHT. LEDS, HOWEVER, ARE VERY EFFICIENT. THEY USE JUST TINY AMOUNTS OF ELECTRICITY.

LED (EHL-EE-DEE) IS SHORT FOR "LIGHT-EMITTING DIODE."

IF YOU LOOK CLOSELY AT AN LED, YOU'LL SEE THAT ONE OF THE WIRES IS A BIT LONGER THAN THE OTHER ONE. THE LONGER ONE IS CALLED THE POSITIVE LEAD (RHYMES WITH "DEED"), THE SHORTER ONE IS THE NEGATIVE LEAD. AS YOU'LL SEE SOON, IT'S IMPORTANT TO KNOW WHICH ONE IS WHICH!

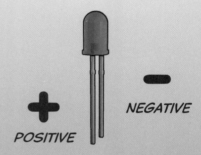

POSITIVE

NEGATIVE

IF YOU ARE NOT SURE WHICH SIDE IS WHICH, LOOK CLOSELY AT THE BOTTOM OF THE LED. IT'S ACTUALLY NOT A PERFECT CIRCLE; INSTEAD, IT HAS A LITTLE FLAT SPOT. THE WIRE CLOSER TO THIS FLAT SPOT IS THE NEGATIVE LEAD.

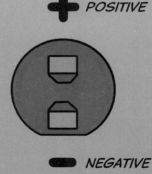

POSITIVE

NEGATIVE

BLINKYBUGS ARE POWERED BY A SMALL COIN-CELL BATTERY. THESE BATTERIES ARE GOOD FOR THINGS THAT USE ONLY A SMALL AMOUNT OF ELECTRICITY, SO THEY WORK GREAT WITH LEDS!

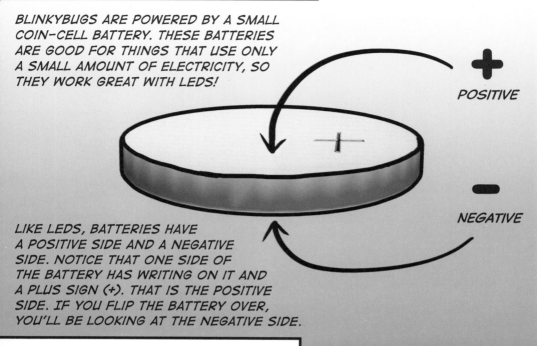

+ POSITIVE

- NEGATIVE

LIKE LEDS, BATTERIES HAVE A POSITIVE SIDE AND A NEGATIVE SIDE. NOTICE THAT ONE SIDE OF THE BATTERY HAS WRITING ON IT AND A PLUS SIGN (+). THAT IS THE POSITIVE SIDE. IF YOU FLIP THE BATTERY OVER, YOU'LL BE LOOKING AT THE NEGATIVE SIDE.

QUICK ACTIVITY: LIGHT UP YOUR LED

TO LEARN HOW THE BATTERY AND LED WORK TOGETHER, FIRST GRAB AN LED AND A BATTERY . . .

. . . AND SLIDE THE LED LEADS OVER THE BATTERY. DID YOUR LED LIGHT UP?

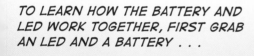

NG LEAD
NTACTS THE
OSITIVE SIDE

SHORT LEAD CONTACTS THE NEGATIVE SIDE

+   **-**

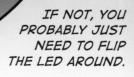

IF NOT, YOU PROBABLY JUST NEED TO FLIP THE LED AROUND.

PIPE CLEANERS

SOMETIMES KNOWN AS "CHENILLE STICKS," THESE BENDY STICKS MAKE EXCELLENT COLORFUL, FUZZY LEGS FOR YOUR BLINKYBUG.

MUSIC WIRE

THIS METAL WIRE IS THE SAME WIRE THAT IS USED FOR GUITAR STRINGS. IT MAKES GREAT BLINKYBUG ANTENNAE (ANN-TEN-NEE, PLURAL OF ANTENNA) BECAUSE IT'S SPRINGY AND IT CON-DUCTS ELECTRICITY. YOU'LL SOON SEE WHY THIS IS VERY IMPORTANT!

COPPER TUBES

YOU WILL USE COPPER TUBES TO ATTACH THE MUSIC-WIRE ANTENNAE TO THE BATTERY.

 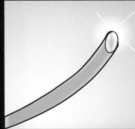

BE CAREFUL WHEN HANDLING MUSIC WIRE—THE ENDS ARE VERY POINTY!

GLUE DOTS

GLUE DOTS WILL STICK TO JUST ABOUT ANYTHING BUT CAN LOSE THEIR STICKI-NESS IF YOU HANDLE THEM TOO MUCH, SO BE CAREFUL TO PICK THEM UP BY THEIR PAPER BACKING!

CONDUCTIVE FOIL TAPE

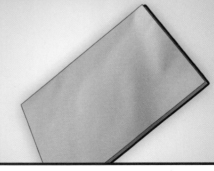

THIS FOIL USES A SPECIAL KIND OF GLUE THAT CONDUCTS ELECTRICITY, SO IT'S GREAT FOR MAKING ELECTRICAL CONNECTIONS BETWEEN THINGS.

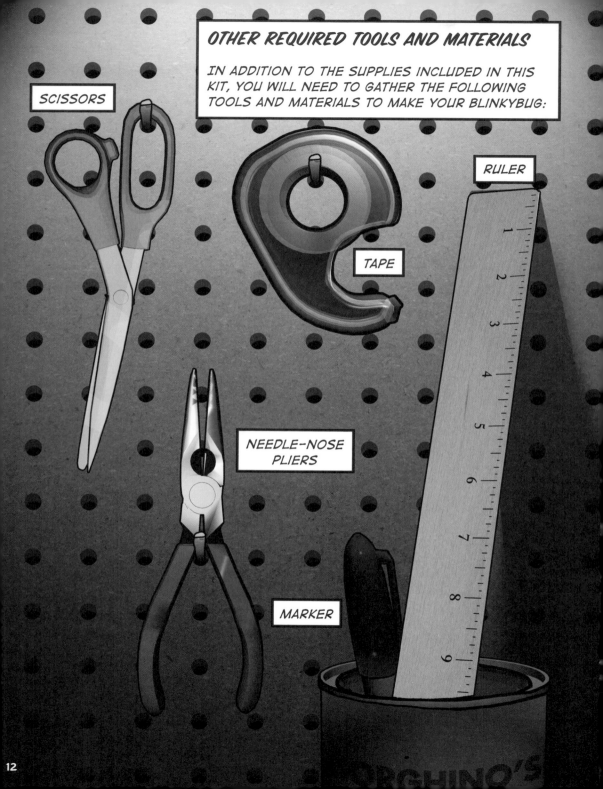

OTHER REQUIRED TOOLS AND MATERIALS

IN ADDITION TO THE SUPPLIES INCLUDED IN THIS KIT, YOU WILL NEED TO GATHER THE FOLLOWING TOOLS AND MATERIALS TO MAKE YOUR BLINKYBUG:

SCISSORS

TAPE

RULER

NEEDLE-NOSE PLIERS

MARKER

PREPARING YOUR WORK AREA

CLEAR A SPACE WITH PLENTY OF LIGHT IN WHICH TO WORK. SOME OF THE SMALL PARTS, SUCH AS THE COPPER TUBES, CAN ROLL AWAY, SO KEEP THEM IN THEIR PACKAGING UNTIL YOU'RE READY TO USE THEM.

STEP 1: PREPARING THE EYES
TO MAKE THE EYES, GRAB TWO LEDS OF THE SAME COLOR.*
NOW GRASP THE LONGER (POSITIVE) LEAD AND BEND IT TO A 90-DEGREE ANGLE. DO THE SAME FOR THE POSITIVE LEAD ON THE OTHER LED, SO THAT BOTH LEDS LOOK THE SAME.
90°
0°
BEND!
*NOTE: YOU CAN USE TWO DIFFERENT-COLORED LEDS, BUT SOME COLORS ACT FUNNY WHEN YOU TRY TO PUT THEM TOGETHER, AND ONLY ONE EYE WILL LIGHT UP AT A TIME!

NEXT YOU'LL ATTACH THE LEDS
TO EACH OTHER BY TWISTING
TOGETHER THE TWO SHORTER
LEADS (THE UNBENT ONES).
TO DO THIS, HOLD ON TO THE
EYES AND CROSS THE SHORTER
LEADS LIKE THIS:

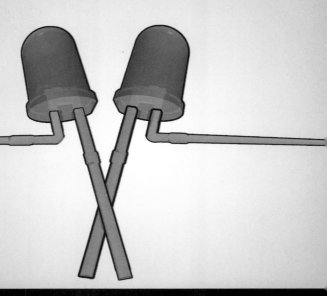

WITH YOUR OTHER HAND,
OR USING PLIERS, GIVE THE
LEADS FOUR TIGHT TWISTS.

YOU SHOULD HAVE SOMETHING
THAT LOOKS LIKE THIS:

TO MAKE SURE EVERYTHING IS NICE
AND TIGHT, USE PLIERS TO GIVE THE
TWISTED LEADS A GOOD SQUEEZE.

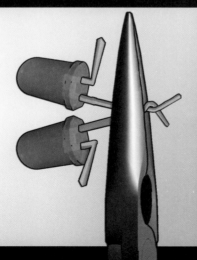

SQUEEEEEEEZE!

YOU'RE DONE PREPARING THE EYES!
YOU CAN PUT THEM ASIDE FOR NOW.

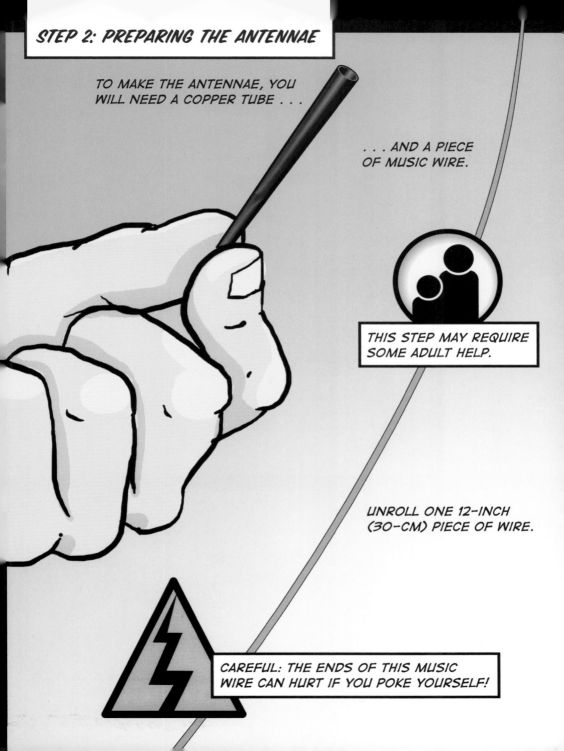

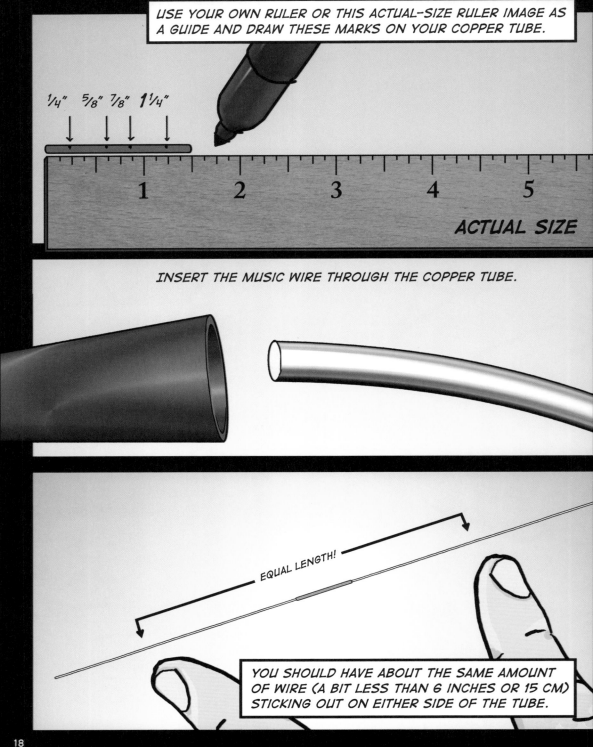

WITH THE TIP OF THE PLIERS, GRAB THE COPPER TUBE BETWEEN THE TWO MARKS YOU MADE IN THE MIDDLE.

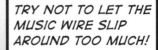

TRY NOT TO LET THE MUSIC WIRE SLIP AROUND TOO MUCH!

THIS STEP MAY REQUIRE SOME ADULT HELP BECAUSE THE TUBE IS HARD TO BEND.

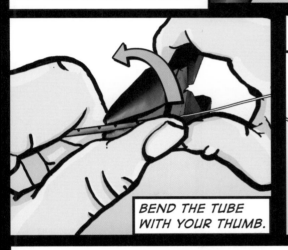

BEND THE TUBE WITH YOUR THUMB.

NOW BEND THE OTHER SIDE WITH YOUR THUMB.

IMPORTANT: IF YOU BEND THE COPPER TUBE IN THE SAME PLACE MORE THAN ONCE, IT MIGHT BREAK!

IT SHOULD NOW LOOK SOMETHING LIKE THIS:

NOW THAT YOU'VE BENT THE COPPER TUBE, THE MUSIC WIRE WON'T SLIP!

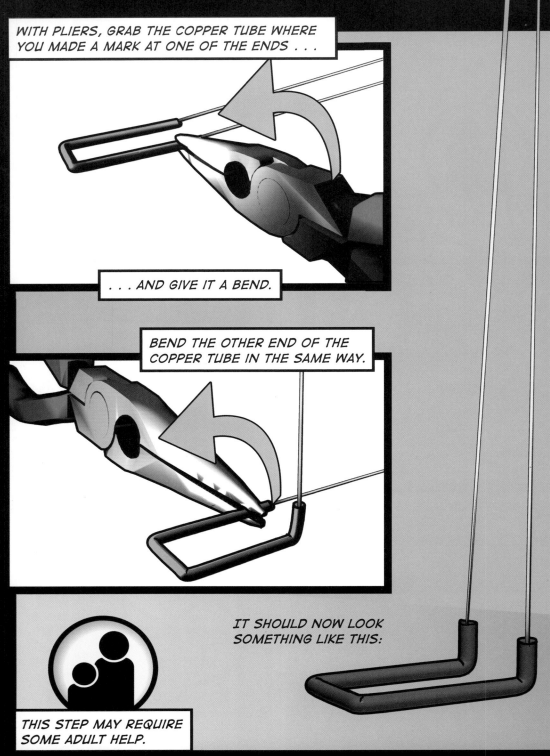

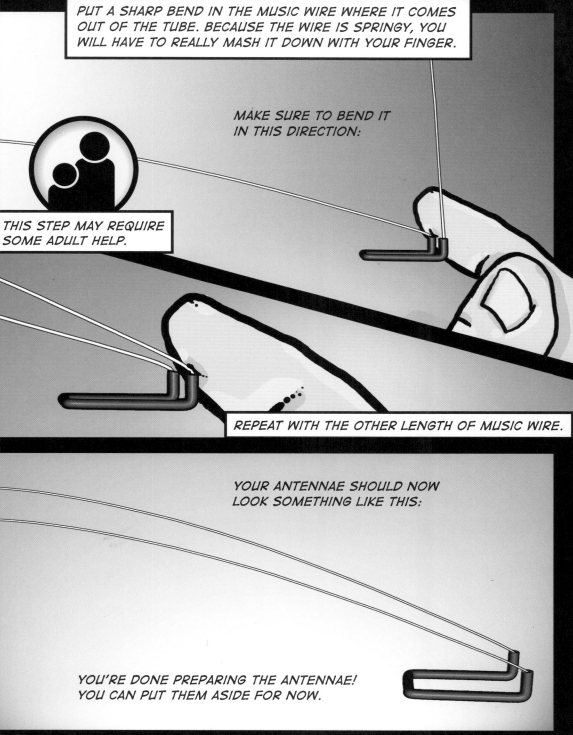

TO ASSEMBLE YOUR BLINKYBUG'S LEGS, FIRST CUT ONE OF THE PIPE CLEANERS INTO THREE 4-INCH (10-CM) PIECES.

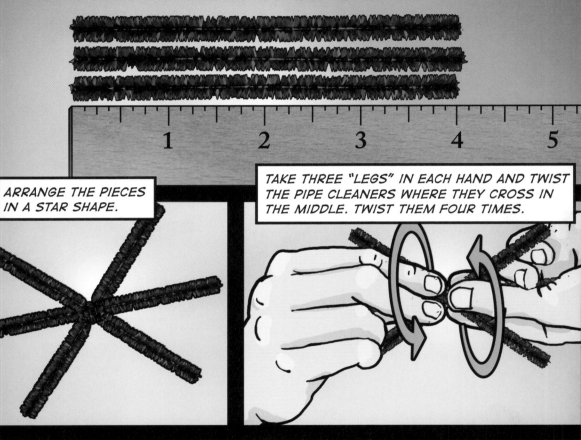

ARRANGE THE PIECES IN A STAR SHAPE.

TAKE THREE "LEGS" IN EACH HAND AND TWIST THE PIPE CLEANERS WHERE THEY CROSS IN THE MIDDLE. TWIST THEM FOUR TIMES.

YOUR BUG'S LEGS SHOULD NOW LOOK SOMETHING LIKE THIS:

YOU'RE DONE ASSEMBLING THE LEGS! YOU CAN PUT THEM ASIDE FOR NOW.

CUT OUT TWO SQUARES OF FOIL IN THE SIZES SHOWN BELOW.

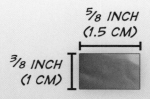

5/8 INCH
(1.5 CM)

3/8 INCH
(1 CM)

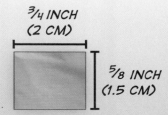

3/4 INCH
(2 CM)

5/8 INCH
(1.5 CM)

FIRST, PRACTICE LINING THINGS UP CORRECTLY.

THE ANTENNAE MUST BE POSITIONED ON THE POSITIVE SIDE OF THE BATTERY!

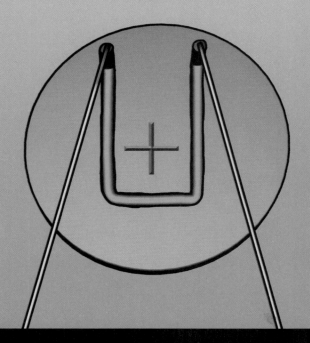

PEEL THE BACKING OFF THE LARGER PIECE OF FOIL.

BE CAREFUL NOT TO TOUCH THE STICKY SIDE, OR IT WILL LOSE ITS STICKINESS!

STICKY SIDE DOWN

ATTACH THE ANTENNAE TO THE POSITIVE SIDE OF THE BATTERY.

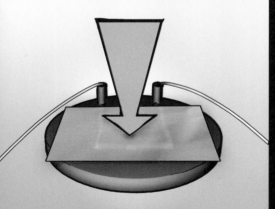

WORKING THE TAPE INTO ALL THE LITTLE NOOKS AND CRANNIES WILL MAKE A STRONGER CONNECTION.

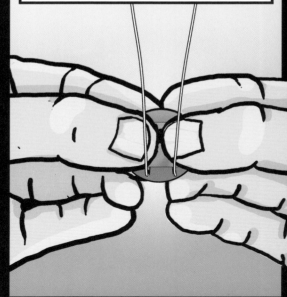

WARNING: DO NOT WRAP THE FOIL AROUND THE BATTERY! IT'S OK IF IT TOUCHES THE EDGES OF THE BATTERY A LITTLE, BUT IT MUST NOT WRAP ALL THE WAY AROUND TO THE OTHER SIDE.

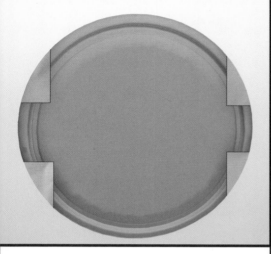

THIS WILL CREATE A SHORT CIRCUIT!*

IF THE FOIL IS TOUCHING THE SIDE OF THE BATTERY, CAREFULLY PEEL THE FOIL BACK AND TRIM IT WITH SCISSORS.

IT SHOULD NOW LOOK SOMETHING LIKE THIS:

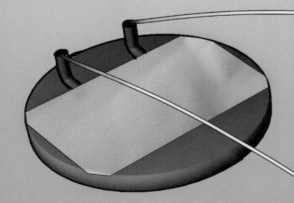

*A **SHORT CIRCUIT** MEANS THAT THE ELECTRICITY IS TRAVELING ALONG THE WRONG PATH. IN THIS CASE, IT MEANS THAT THE ELECTRICITY IS FLOWING FROM THE POSITIVE SIDE OF THE BATTERY TO THE NEGATIVE SIDE WITHOUT FLOWING THROUGH THE LED. THIS WILL PREVENT THE LEDS FROM LIGHTING UP, AND IT WILL QUICKLY DRAIN THE BATTERY.

BEFORE YOU ATTACH THE LEDS TO THE BODY, MAKE SURE YOU KNOW HOW THEY SHOULD LINE UP. THE TWISTED LED LEADS WILL ATTACH TO THE NEGATIVE SIDE OF THE BATTERY, AND THE EYES NEED TO POINT IN THE SAME DIRECTION AS THE ANTENNAE, WITH THE LED LEADS POINTING UP, LIKE THIS:

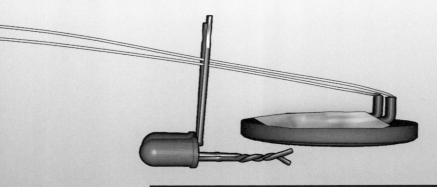

IMPORTANT: MAKE SURE THE NEGATIVE LED LEADS DO NOT TOUCH THE EDGES OF THE BATTERY! THE EDGES ARE ACTUALLY CONNECTED TO THE POSITIVE SIDE OF THE BATTERY, SO THAT WOULD CREATE A SHORT CIRCUIT!

PEEL THE BACKING OFF THE SMALLER PIECE OF FOIL. HOLDING THE EYES BY ONE OF THE POSITIVE LEADS . . .

. . . PLACE THE FOIL WHERE THE TWISTED LEADS FORM A "Y."

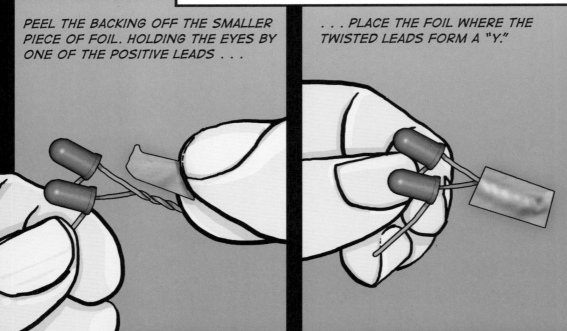

ATTACH THE LEDS TO THE BATTERY, WORKING THE FOIL INTO THE NOOKS AND CRANNIES.

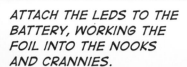

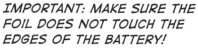

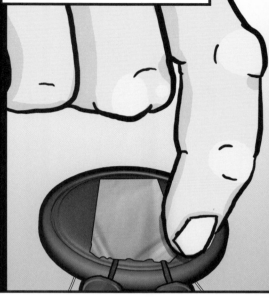

IF YOU HAVE THIS PROBLEM, CAREFULLY PEEL THE FOIL BACK A LITTLE WITH YOUR FINGERNAIL OR TRIM THE FOIL WITH SCISSORS.

FROM THE FRONT, IT SHOULD NOW LOOK SOMETHING LIKE THIS:

FROM THE SIDE, YOUR BLINKYBUG SHOULD NOW LOOK SOMETHING LIKE THIS:

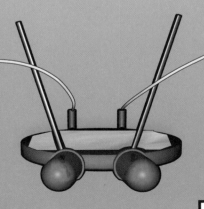

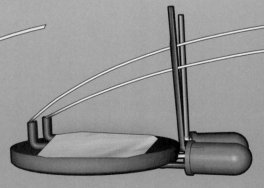

IF SOMETHING DOESN'T QUITE MATCH, JUST PEEL OFF THE FOIL AND TRY AGAIN. IF THE FOIL LOSES ITS STICKINESS, DON'T WORRY; THERE IS EXTRA FOIL IN YOUR KIT.

YOUR BLINKYBUG'S LED EYES MAY ALREADY BE
BLINKING OR EVEN SEEM LIKE THEY'RE STUCK ON.
DON'T WORRY ABOUT THAT . . . YOU'LL FINE-TUNE
EVERYTHING LATER. IF THE EYES ARE NOT LIT UP YET,
GENTLY BEND ONE OF THE ANTENNAE WIRES SO
THAT IT BRIEFLY TOUCHES ONE OF THE LED LEADS.

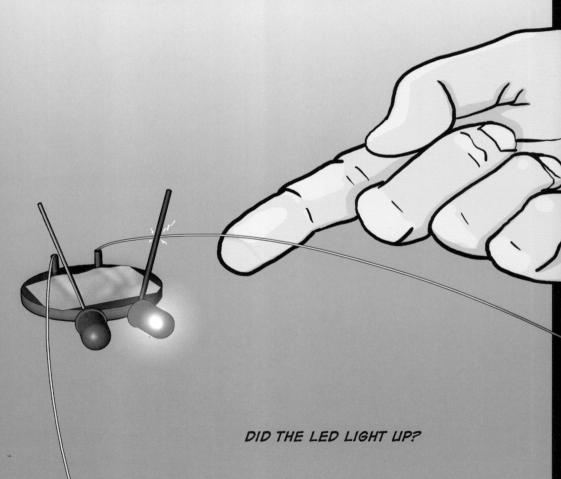

DID THE LED LIGHT UP?

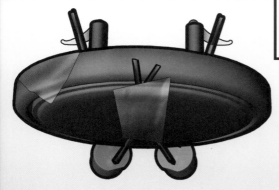

IF YOUR BLINKYBUG'S EYES ARE NOT BLINKING, HERE ARE A FEW THINGS TO TRY:

LOOK FOR SHORT CIRCUITS. ARE THE NEGATIVE (TWISTED) LED LEADS TOUCHING THE EDGE OF THE BATTERY? IS THE FOIL ON THE BOTTOM TOUCHING THE SIDES OF THE BATTERY OR IS THE FOIL ON TOP WRAPPING ALL THE WAY AROUND TO THE OTHER SIDE?

CHECK TO SEE IF THE LEDS ARE BACKWARD. IT'S EASY TO ACCIDENTALLY TWIST THE POSITIVE LEADS TOGETHER INSTEAD OF THE NEGATIVE ONES. LOOK CLOSELY AT THE LEDS: THE LITTLE FLAT SPOT ON THE PLASTIC LENS SHOULD **NOT** BE ON THE SAME SIDE OF THE BATTERY AS THE ANTENNAE. IF IT'S BACKWARD, THERE'S AN EASY FIX—REMOVE THE ANTENNAE AND EYES FROM THE BATTERY AND REATTACH THEM SO THAT THE ANTENNAE ARE ATTACHED TO THE NEGATIVE SIDE OF THE BATTERY AND THE EYES ARE ATTACHED TO THE POSITIVE SIDE OF THE BATTERY.

REVERSED!

NEGATIVE LEAD

IF ALL ELSE FAILS, CAREFULLY REMOVE THE EYES AND ANTENNAE FROM THE BATTERY AND REATTACH THEM WITH FRESH PIECES OF ADHESIVE FOIL. THIS WILL OFTEN DO THE TRICK.

IF ONLY ONE LED LIGHTS UP AT A TIME:

AS MENTIONED EARLIER, SOMETIMES DIFFERENTLY COLORED LEDS BEHAVE STRANGELY WHEN PAIRED UP. THIS HAS TO DO WITH THE FACT THAT DIFFERENTLY COLORED LEDS REQUIRE DIFFERENT VOLTAGES (IN SIMPLE TERMS, THE FORCE OF THE FLOW OF ELECTRICITY). WHEN THE VOLTAGES DON'T MATCH, ONE LED CAN STEAL THE ELECTRICITY AWAY FROM THE OTHER ONE! IF YOU HAVE A BLINKYBUG THAT BEHAVES THIS WAY, DON'T WORRY ABOUT IT . . . THINK OF IT AS A UNIQUE CHARACTERISTIC!

ADJUSTING YOUR BLINKYBUG

AS MENTIONED EARLIER (SEE PAGE 5), THE CONTACT BETWEEN THE ANTENNAE WIRE AND THE LED LEADS CAUSES YOUR BLINKYBUG'S EYES TO LIGHT UP.

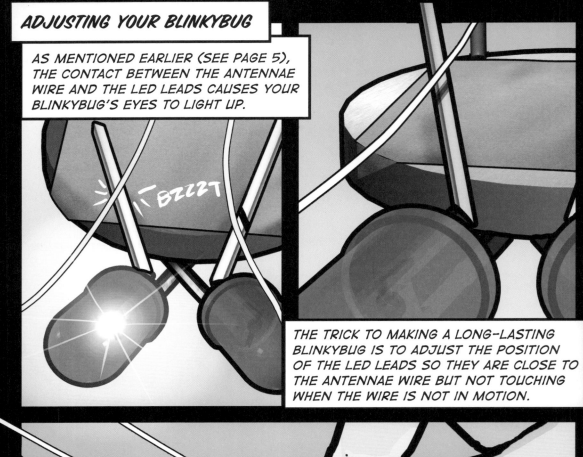

BZZZT

THE TRICK TO MAKING A LONG-LASTING BLINKYBUG IS TO ADJUST THE POSITION OF THE LED LEADS SO THEY ARE CLOSE TO THE ANTENNAE WIRE BUT NOT TOUCHING WHEN THE WIRE IS NOT IN MOTION.

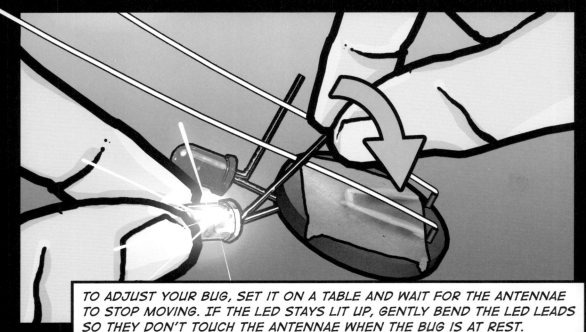

TO ADJUST YOUR BUG, SET IT ON A TABLE AND WAIT FOR THE ANTENNAE TO STOP MOVING. IF THE LED STAYS LIT UP, GENTLY BEND THE LED LEADS SO THEY DON'T TOUCH THE ANTENNAE WHEN THE BUG IS AT REST.

STEP 6: ATTACHING THE ANENNAE

YOU'RE ALMOST DONE! TO ATTACH THE LEGS, YOU'LL NEED ONE OF THE GLUE DOTS INCLUDED IN THIS KIT.

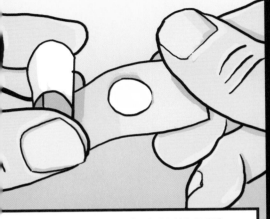

WHEN HANDLING THE GLUE DOT, HOLD ON TO THE PAPER. TOUCHING THE GLUE DOT TOO MUCH WILL CAUSE IT TO LOSE ITS STICKINESS.

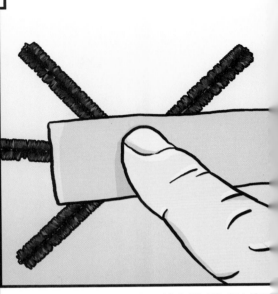

LAY THE ASSEMBLED LEGS FLAT ON THE TABLE, AND PRESS THE GLUE DOT, STICK SIDE DOWN, INTO THE PLACE WHERE TH LEGS ARE TWISTED TOGETHER.

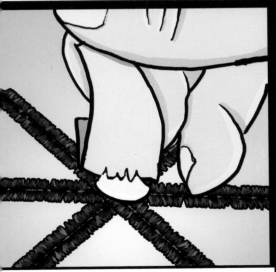

CAREFULLY PEEL THE PAPER BACKING AWAY FROM THE GLUE DOT. THE GLUE DOT SHOULD STAY STUCK TO THE LEGS—YOU MAY NEED TO GIVE IT A LITTLE NUDGE TO HELP IT STICK.

STICK THE LEGS TO YOUR BLINKYBUG'S BELLY.

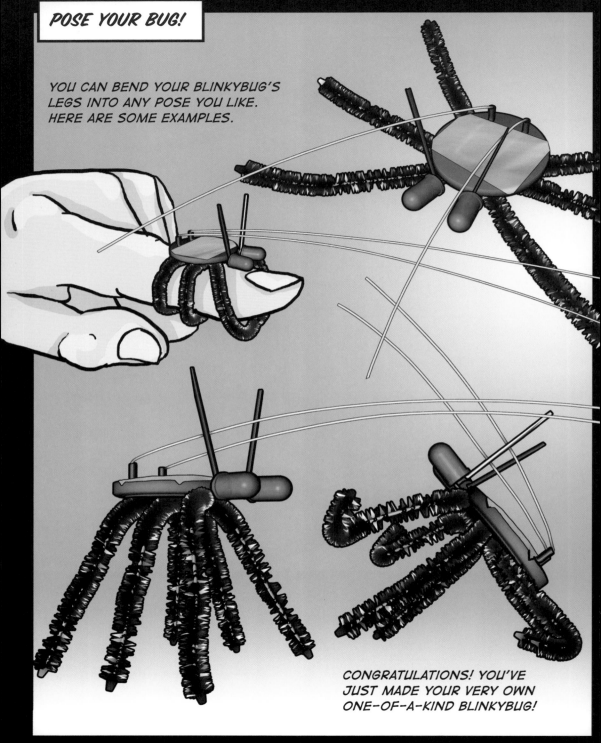

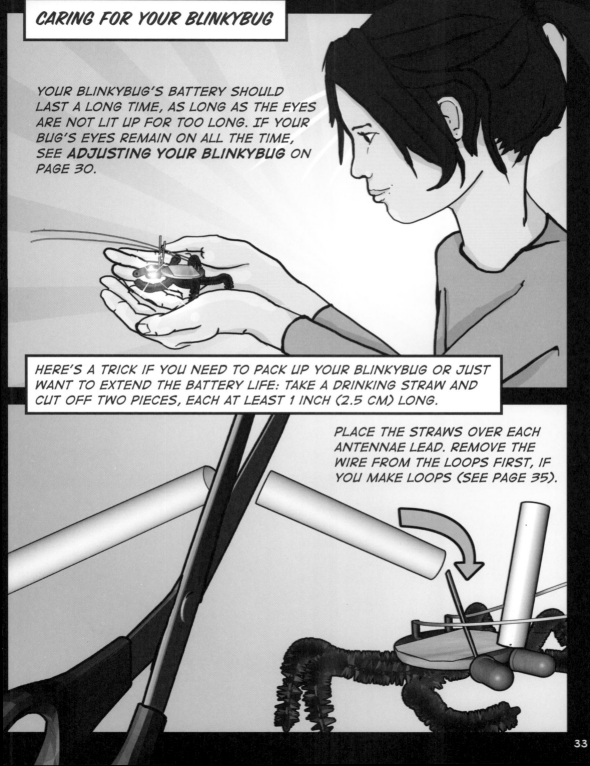

CARING FOR YOUR BLINKYBUG

YOUR BLINKYBUG'S BATTERY SHOULD LAST A LONG TIME, AS LONG AS THE EYES ARE NOT LIT UP FOR TOO LONG. IF YOUR BUG'S EYES REMAIN ON ALL THE TIME, SEE *ADJUSTING YOUR BLINKYBUG* ON PAGE 30.

HERE'S A TRICK IF YOU NEED TO PACK UP YOUR BLINKYBUG OR JUST WANT TO EXTEND THE BATTERY LIFE: TAKE A DRINKING STRAW AND CUT OFF TWO PIECES, EACH AT LEAST 1 INCH (2.5 CM) LONG.

PLACE THE STRAWS OVER EACH ANTENNAE LEAD. REMOVE THE WIRE FROM THE LOOPS FIRST, IF YOU MAKE LOOPS (SEE PAGE 35).

SPECIAL FEATURES FOR YOUR BLINKYBUG

IF YOU'D LIKE TO MAKE YOUR BLINKYBUG
MORE SENSITIVE TO WIND, YOU CAN ADD LITTLE
FLAPS TO THE ENDS OF THE ANTENNAE. TAKE
A SMALL PIECE (ABOUT 1 INCH OR 2.5 CM) OF
CELLOPHANE TAPE AND FOLD IT OVER THE END
OF ONE ANTENNA.

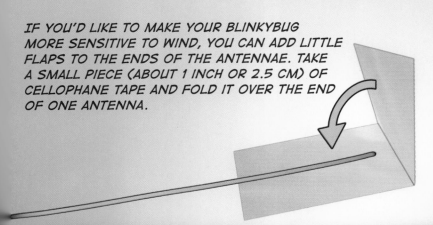

TRIM THE EDGES OF THE TAPE.

YOUR BLINKYBUG'S
ANTENNA FLAP SHOULD
NOW LOOK SOMETHING
LIKE THIS:

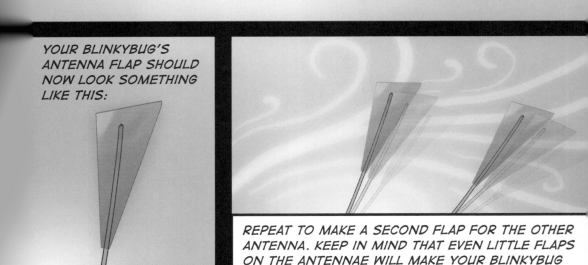

REPEAT TO MAKE A SECOND FLAP FOR THE OTHER
ANTENNA. KEEP IN MIND THAT EVEN LITTLE FLAPS
ON THE ANTENNAE WILL MAKE YOUR BLINKYBUG
MUCH MORE SENSITIVE TO THE WIND!

LED LEAD LOOPS

YOUR BLINKYBUG SHOULD BLINK BEAUTIFULLY AS IT IS, BUT IF YOU WANT TO GIVE IT A LITTLE EXTRA BLINKYNESS, YOU CAN ADD LITTLE LOOPS TO THE END OF THE LED LEADS. USE PLIERS TO GRAB THE TIP OF A LEAD . . .

THIS STEP MAY REQUIRE SOME ADULT HELP.

GAP!

. . . AND GENTLY BEND THE END OUTWARD INTO A SMALL LOOP, MAKING SURE TO LEAVE A LITTLE GAP FOR THE ANTENNAE.

REPEAT WITH THE OTHER LED, SO IT NOW LOOKS SOMETHING LIKE THIS:

SLIP THE ANTENNA WIRE THROUGH THE GAP IN EACH LOOP.

YOU MAY NEED TO READJUST THE POSITION OF THE LOOPED LEADS SO THAT WHEN THE ANTENNAE AREN'T MOVING, THEY PASS THROUGH THE LOOPS WITHOUT TOUCHING.

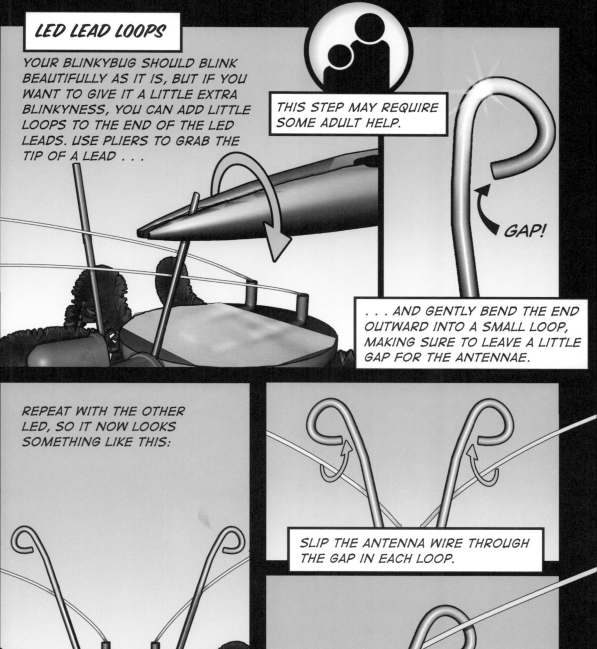

YOU'VE SEEN HOW THE MOTION
OF THE ANTENNAE . . .

. . . AND THE CONTACT
BETWEEN THE WIRES
MAKES YOUR BLINKY-
BUG'S EYES LIGHT UP.

WHAT IS REALLY GOING ON HERE?

LET'S LOOK AT ALL THE BUG PARTS PUT TOGETHER.

THE ELECTRICITY USES THE ANTENNA WIRE AS A PATHWAY TO GET TO THE LEDS. ALL OF THESE PARTS TOGETHER MAKE UP AN **ELECTRICAL CIRCUIT**.

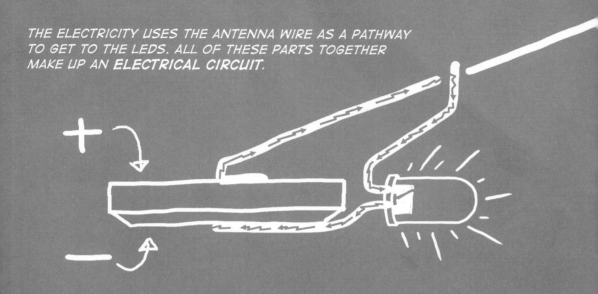

HERE IS A REALLY SIMPLE CIRCUIT. IN ORDER FOR ELECTRICITY TO FLOW TO THE LIGHTBULB, THE CIRCUIT MUST BE **COMPLETE**. THAT IS, IT MUST MAKE A COMPLETE LOOP THAT GOES ALL THE WAY FROM THE POSITIVE (+) SIDE OF THE BATTERY TO THE NEGATIVE (–) SIDE.

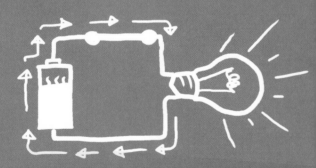

IN THIS CIRCUIT, THE SWITCH IS **OPEN** (JUST LIKE WHEN YOUR BLINKYBUG'S WIRES ARE NOT TOUCHING). THIS PREVENTS ANY ELECTRICITY FROM FLOWING THROUGH THE CIRCUIT.

NOW THE SWITCH IS **CLOSED**, SO THE ELECTRICAL CURRENT CAN FLOW THROUGH THE CIRCUIT, LIGHTING UP THE LED ON ITS WAY!

LEDS ARE NOT LIGHTBULBS! WHILE BOTH LEDS AND LIGHTBULBS DO A GREAT JOB OF TURNING ELECTRICAL ENERGY INTO LIGHT, INCANDESCENT LIGHT-BULBS* ALSO PRODUCE A LOT OF HEAT. THE PROBLEM IS THAT ALL THAT HEAT IS ACTUALLY WASTED ENERGY! BECAUSE OF ALL THAT WASTED ENERGY, A BRIGHT LIGHTBULB NEEDS TO USE A LOT OF ENERGY TO STAY LIT.

LEDS, ON THE OTHER HAND, ARE VERY EFFICIENT. THEY PRODUCE VERY LITTLE HEAT, SO ALMOST ALL OF THE ENERGY THEY USE IS TURNED INTO LIGHT. THIS IS HOW WE GET AWAY WITH USING SUCH TINY LITTLE BATTERIES.

*INCANDESCENT LIGHTBULBS ARE THE KIND YOU USUALLY FIND AROUND THE HOUSE, ALTHOUGH THEY'RE BEING REPLACED MORE AND MORE WITH ENERGY-SAVING COMPACT FLUORESCENT LIGHTS.

A HOME FOR YOUR BLINKYBUGS

. . . OR IT CAN SIT ON YOUR DESK.

PUT YOUR BLINKYBUG NEAR A FAN SO IT WILL BLINK IN THE BREEZE.

YOUR BLINKYBUG CAN SIT ON A WINDOWSILL . . .

YOU CAN ALSO MAKE A HOME FOR YOUR BLINKYBUG INSIDE A CARDBOARD BOX.

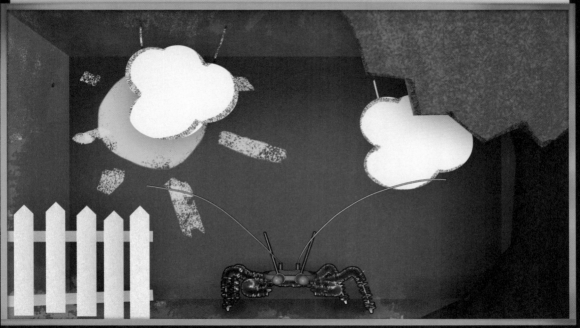

BLINKYBUGS AND BEYOND

NOW THAT YOU'VE LEARNED THE ART OF BLINKYBUG BUILDING,
WHAT OTHER CREATIVE CREATURES CAN YOU COME UP WITH?
HERE ARE SOME IDEAS TO GET YOU STARTED.

FLYING BLINKYBUG

MAKE A MAGNIFICENT FLYING BLINKY-
BUG WITH YOUR FAVORITE COLORS!

ATTACH FEATHERS AND POM-POMS TO THE BATTERY WITH CRAFT GLUE.

UNIQUE COLORED FEATHERS, SMALL MAGNETS, PIN BACKINGS,
AND MORE CAN BE FOUND AT HOBBY AND ARTS AND CRAFTS
SHOPS IN YOUR NEIGHBORHOOD OR ONLINE.

MAGNETIC BLINKYBUG

ATTACH A MAGNET TO THE BOTTOM OF A BLINKYBUG WITH CRAFT GLUE OR AN EXTRA GLUE DOT.

PUT THIS BUGGY REMINDER RIGHT ON THE FRIDGE!

BLINKYBUG JEWELRY

CREATE YOUR OWN SIGNATURE BLINKYBUG JEWELRY!

ATTACH A PIN BACKING WITH CRAFT GLUE OR AN EXTRA GLUE DOT.

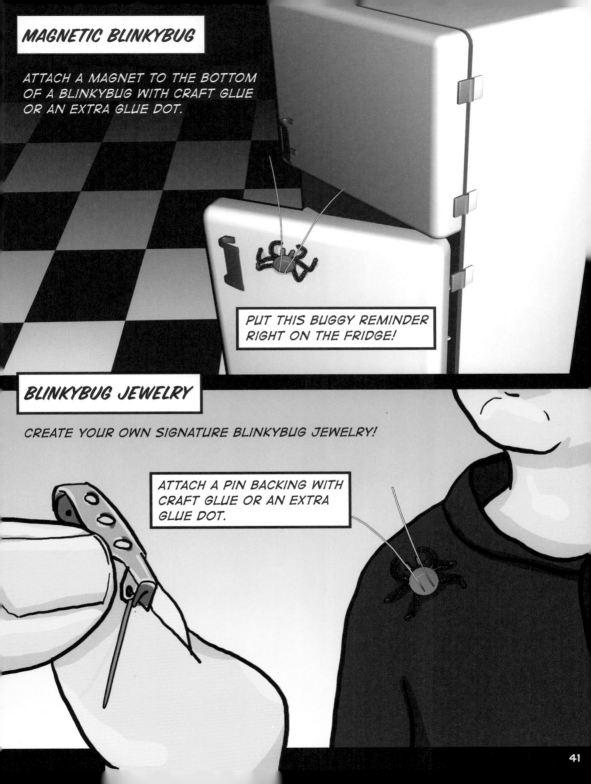

BLINK-ANTULA

ATTACH A POM-POM TO THE TOP OF THE REAR LEGS WITH CRAFT GLUE.

BEND AN EXTRA PIPE CLEANER LIKE SO:

ATTACH THE PIPE CLEANER BELOW THE EYES TO MAKE MANDIBLES (THE SPIDER'S MOUTH).

BLINKYWORM

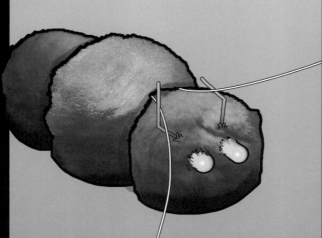

THIS CRAWLY CREATURE REQUIRES USING THE POM-POMS IN YOUR KIT ALONG WITH A NEEDLE AND THREAD.

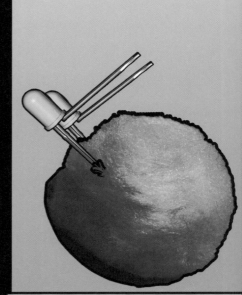

BEFORE TWISTING THE LEDS TOGETHER, POKE THE NEGATIVE (UNBENT) LEADS THROUGH A POM-POM . . .

. . . AND TWIST THEM TOGETHER ON THE OTHER SIDE.

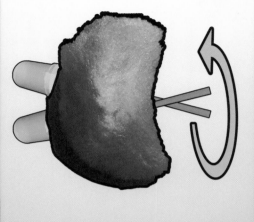

ATTACH THE BATTERY WITH FOIL TAPE.

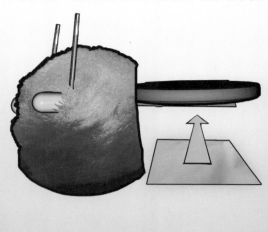

BEND THE BATTERY DOWN LIKE THIS TO HIDE IT BETWEEN THE POM-POMS.

THIS STEP MAY REQUIRE SOME ADULT HELP.

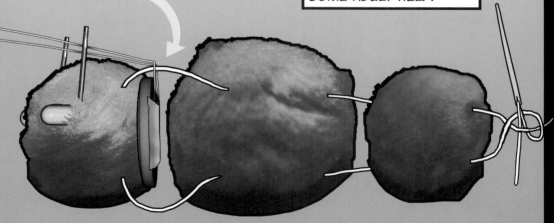

POKE THE NEEDLE AND THREAD THROUGH EACH POM-POM AND THEN PULL THEM SNUGLY TOGETHER.

BLINKY-BOT

THIS GUY OR GAL IS MADE FROM MODELING CLAY.

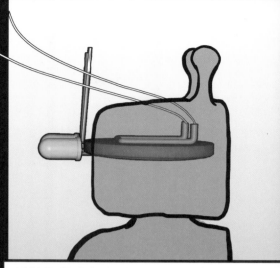

MOLD THE CLAY AROUND THE BATTERY TO FORM THE BLINKY-BOT'S HEAD.

HERE ARE PHOTOS OF SOME OF THESE BLINKY CREATIONS FOR YOUR INSPIRATION!

FIRST, MAKE A BLINKYBUG, BUT DON'T ATTACH ANY LEGS!

SCIENCE PROJECTS WITH YOUR BLINKYBUGS

EXPERIMENT: HOW DOES LENGTH AFFECT BLINKING SPEED?

BUILD A BLINKYBUG WITH ANTENNAE OF DIFFERENT LENGTHS. FOR THE MOST VISIBLE RESULTS, MAKE ONE ANTENNA ABOUT TWICE AS LONG AS THE OTHER.

THE RATE THAT THE LEDS BLINK IS CALLED THEIR FREQUENCY.

GIVE YOUR BUG A SHAKE. DOES ONE EYE BLINK FASTER THAN THE OTHER? WHICH ONE? CAN YOU FIGURE OUT WHY?

WHAT'S GOING ON HERE?

THE LONGER THE ANTENNA (OR, THE MORE "MASS" IT HAS), THE SLOWER IT MOVES BACK AND FORTH. THIS MOVEMENT IS CALLED OSCILLATION. SO, A LONGER ANTENNA WILL OSCILLATE MORE SLOWLY THAN A SHORTER ONE, CAUSING THE EYE THAT'S CONNECTED TO THE LONGER ANTENNA TO BLINK MORE SLOWLY.

LOTS OF THINGS OSCILLATE. FOR EXAMPLE:

A STRING ON A MUSICAL INSTRUMENT, LIKE A GUITAR OR VIOLIN. THESE STRINGS OSCILLATE MUCH FASTER THAN A BLINKYBUG'S ANTENNAE.

A PENDULUM (LIKE IN A GRANDFATHER CLOCK). THE MORE IT WEIGHS, THE SLOWER IT MOVES.

EXPERIMENT: WHICH MATERIALS CONDUCT ELECTRICITY?

YOU CAN BUILD A SPECIAL BLINKYBUG THAT CAN SENSE WHETHER OR NOT SOMETHING CONDUCTS ELECTRICITY. YOU'LL NEED SOME EXTRA PARTS, WHICH YOU CAN FIND AT A HARDWARE STORE OR HOBBY SHOP (OR ONLINE). YOU'LL NEED:

- A SMALL SPOOL OF 22-GAUGE STRANDED WIRE
- ONE "MINI" ALLIGATOR CLIP
- WIRE-CUTTERS AND STRIPPERS
- NEEDLE-NOSE PLIERS

ADULT HELP IS NECESSARY FOR THIS PROCEDURE.

1. FOLLOW THE DIRECTIONS YOU'LL FIND ON **WWW.CHRONICLEBOOKS.COM/ BLINKYBUG** TO BUILD A CONDUCTIVITY-DETECTING BLINKYBUG.
2. TO TEST WHETHER A MATERIAL CONDUCTS ELECTRICITY, ATTACH THE CLIP TO IT, THEN TOUCH THE MATERIAL WITH THE LED LEADS. SEE IF YOUR BLINKY-BUG'S EYES LIGHT UP.

IF THE EYES LIGHT UP, THE MATERIAL CONDUCTS ELECTRICITY.

THIS IS A COMPLETE CIRCUIT. IF THE FORK DID NOT CONDUCT ELECTRICITY, THE CIRCUIT WOULD NOT BE COMPLETE, AND THE EYES WOULD NOT TURN ON.

3. TEST MATERIALS. WHICH DO YOU THINK WILL CONDUCT ELECTRICITY?

- SILVER UTENSIL
- STAINLESS STEEL UTENSIL
- PLASTIC UTENSIL
- GOLD JEWELRY
- BRASS FAUCET HANDLE
- PAPER CLIP

- GLASS
- CLAY POT
- COPPER POT OR DISH
- SPONGE
- COIN
- ALUMINUM FOIL

- COMPACT DISC
- PAPER OR WOOD
- WAX CANDLE
- LEAF
- IRON SKILLET

CAUTION: IT IS SAFE TO USE YOUR BLINKYBUG IN THE WAY DESCRIBED HERE, BUT NEVER CONNECT IT TO ANYTHING THAT USES ELECTRICITY OR IS PLUGGED INTO AN ELECTRICAL OUTLET. THIS CAN BE EXTREMELY DANGEROUS.

WHAT'S GOING ON HERE?

WHAT DECIDES WHETHER A MATERIAL CONDUCTS ELECTRICITY? IT HAS TO DO WITH ITS ELECTRONS AND HOW THEY ARE ARRANGED AROUND THE NUCLEI OF ITS ATOMS. HINT: METALS TEND TO HAVE THE RIGHT ARRANGE-MENT! TO FIND OUT MORE, RESEARCH "ELECTRICAL CONDUCTIVITY."

WHAT'S NEXT?

WHAT OTHER BLINKY CREATIONS CAN YOU THINK OF? WHAT KINDS OF MATERIALS CAN YOU FIND OR RECYCLE TO MAKE YOUR BLINKY CREATURES TRULY UNIQUE? THE BEST PLACE TO LOOK WILL BE YOUR OWN IMAGINATION!